SPOTLIGHT ON GEORGIA

GEORGIA AND THE MODERN CIVIL RIGHTS MOVEMENT

SAM CROMPTON

PowerKiDS press.

NEW YORK

Published in 2018 by The Rosen Publishing Group, Inc.
29 East 21st Street, New York, NY 10010

Editor: Theresa Morlock
Book Design: Michael Flynn

Photo Credits: Cover, pp. 13, 27 Bettmann/Bettmann/Getty Images; p. 5 Forty3Zero/Shutterstock.com; p. 6 Everett Historical/Shutterstock.com; p. 7 https://commons.wikimedia.org/wiki/File:JimCrowInDurhamNC.jpg; p. 9 (background) Reinhold Leitner/Shutterstock.com; p. 9 (document) National Archives and Records Administration, Records of the Supreme Court, Record Group 267, National Archives Identifier: 301669; p. 11 Erik S. Lesser/Hulton Archive/Getty Images; p. 14 Robert W. Kelley/The LIFE Picture Collection/Getty Images; pp. 15, 19 Don Cravens/The LIFE Images Collection/Getty Images; p. 17 Afro Newspaper/Gado/Archive Photos/Getty Images; p. 20 -/Stringer/AFP/Getty Images; p. 21 National Archives/Handout/Hulton Archive/Getty Images; p. 23 https://commons.wikimedia.org/wiki/File:Lyndon_Johnson_signing_Civil_Rights_Act,_July_2,_1964.jpg; p. 25 Francis Miller/The LIFE Picture Collection/Getty Images; p. 26 Underwood Archives/Archive Photos/Getty Images; p. 29 Paul Schutzer/The LIFE Picture Collection/Getty Images.

Cataloging-in-Publication Data
Names: Crompton, Sam.
Title: Georgia and the modern civil rights movement / Sam Crompton.
Description: New York : PowerKids Press, 2018. | Series: Spotlight on Georgia | Includes index.
Identifiers: ISBN 9781508159766 (pbk.) | ISBN 9781508159797 (library bound) | ISBN 9781508159773 (6 pack)
Subjects: LCSH: African Americans--Civil rights--Georgia--History--20th century--Juvenile literature. | Civil rights movements--Georgia--Juvenile literature. | Georgia--History--Juvenile literature.
Classification: LCC E185.61 C76 2018 | DDC 323.1196'07307580904--dc23

Manufactured in the United States of America

CPSIA Compliance Information: Batch #BS17PK For further information contact Rosen Publishing, New York, New York at 1-800-237-9932.

CONTENTS

CHAPTER ONE

THE CIVIL RIGHTS MOVEMENT

During the American civil rights movement of the mid-1950s to the late 1960s, **activists** fought a long, tough battle to gain equal rights. African Americans sought to end **segregation** and **discrimination** and gain the same employment, education, and housing opportunities white people had.

At this time, conditions for African Americans in Georgia were among the worst in the South. Georgia had once been a slave state, and many white people still believed they were superior to other races. African American Georgians dealt with abuse from their fellow citizens on a daily basis. **White supremacist** leaders prevented African American Georgians from voting, used violence against them, and tried to keep segregation in place.

During the civil rights movement, Georgia became a hot spot for activism. Civil rights protests, marches, and legal cases took place across the state, gaining national news attention.

Martin Luther King Jr., one of the most famous civil rights leaders, was from Atlanta, Georgia. This mural is located at Martin Luther King Jr. National Historic Site in Atlanta.

CHAPTER TWO

JIM CROW LAWS

The 14th Amendment of 1868 granted all American citizens equal protection under the law. This was one of several amendments approved after the Civil War that were designed to ensure equal rights for African Americans. However, many southern states **enacted** their own state laws to limit these rights and **enforce** segregation. These discriminatory southern state laws came to be called Jim Crow laws.

Jim Crow was a fictional black character created by a white actor in the 1830s. "Jim Crow" became a disrespectful term used to describe African Americans.

Jim Crow laws in Georgia made it illegal for white and African American people to marry each other. Jim Crow laws also required that many sites and businesses—including parks, restaurants, liquor stores, barber shops, and hospitals—be segregated. African American Georgians were denied voting rights and refused access to public **facilities**. They were often victims of racial violence. Jim Crow laws were in effect for years. Many were not challenged until the rise of the civil rights movement in the 1950s.

CHAPTER THREE

BROWN V. BOARD OF EDUCATION

Brown v. Board of Education was a court case filed by Oliver Brown, a black man, against the Topeka, Kansas, school board. Brown's daughter wasn't allowed to attend a white school in Topeka. Under law, segregated facilities such as schools had to be of equal quality. Brown said that denying his child access to the white school was illegal because the white and black schools in Topeka weren't equal. The case went all the way to the Supreme Court. In May 1954, the court, under Chief Justice Earl Warren, decided that racial segregation of children in public schools was unconstitutional.

Although the *Brown v. Board of Education* decision didn't end segregation, it was an important step toward putting federal law on the side of racial equality. After the *Brown v. Board of Education* decision, schools in Georgia began to become integrated, which means they were no longer segregated by race.

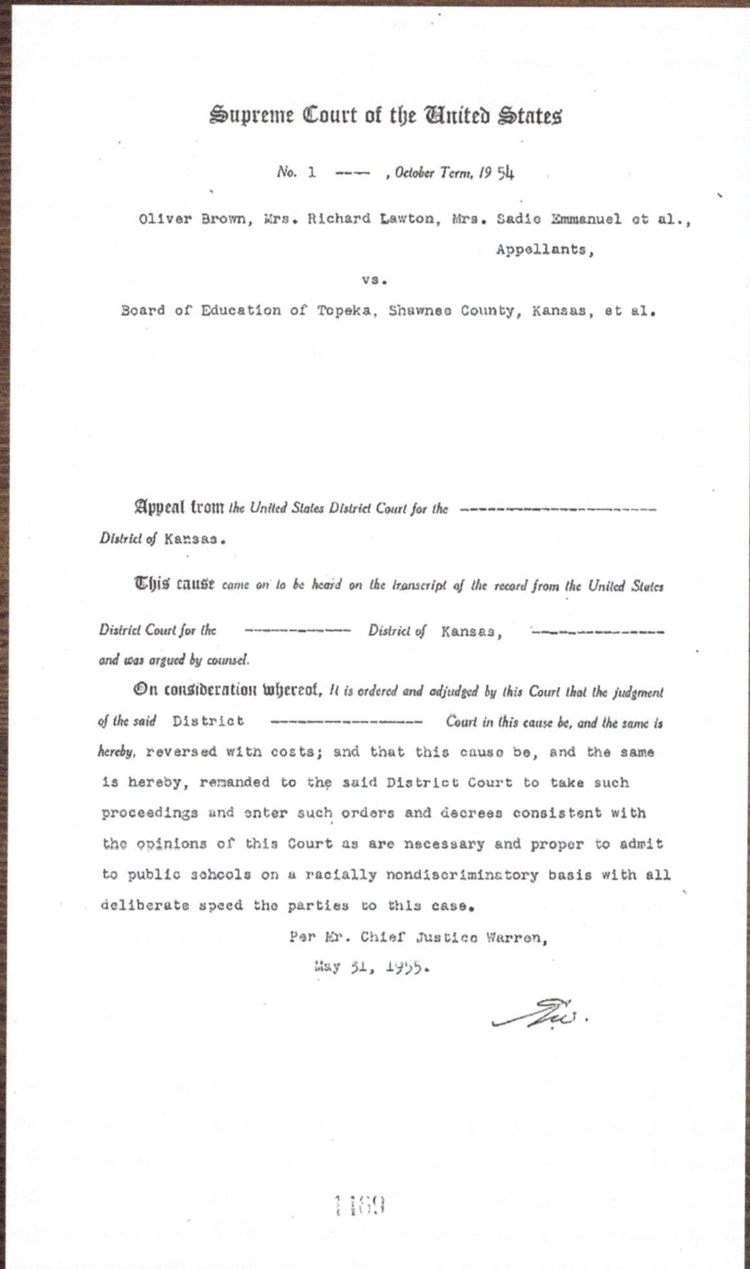
Supreme Court of the United States

No. 1 ---- , October Term, 19 54

Oliver Brown, Mrs. Richard Lawton, Mrs. Sadie Emmanuel et al.,
Appellants,

vs.

Board of Education of Topeka, Shawnee County, Kansas, et al.

Appeal from the United States District Court for the ----------------------
District of Kansas.

This cause came on to be heard on the transcript of the record from the United States District Court for the ------------ District of Kansas, ------------ and was argued by counsel.

On consideration whereof, It is ordered and adjudged by this Court that the judgment of the said District --------------- Court in this cause be, and the same is hereby, reversed with costs; and that this cause be, and the same is hereby, remanded to the said District Court to take such proceedings and enter such orders and decrees consistent with the opinions of this Court as are necessary and proper to admit to public schools on a racially nondiscriminatory basis with all deliberate speed the parties to this case.

Per Mr. Chief Justice Warren,
May 31, 1955.

1469

This document is the Supreme Court record of the *Brown v. Board of Education* case. The court decided that segregated schools were not equal because African American students weren't given the same opportunities as white children.

CHAPTER FOUR

THE 1956 STATE FLAG

The *Brown v. Board of Education* decision was not easily accepted in Georgia. Lawmakers enacted state laws to keep segregation in place. The government approved a plan for segregated private schools so that if the federal government forced integration in public schools, the public schools could simply be closed. Many Georgians in favor of segregation felt that the federal government was overstepping its bounds by interfering with the way the state government dealt with its citizens.

To symbolize the state's rejection of desegregation, Georgia adopted a new state flag in 1956. The new Georgia flag showed the stars and bars of the Confederate flag. During the Civil War, the Confederacy was composed of states that fought to keep slavery. By adopting a flag that resembled the Confederate flag, the state's politicians sent a message that Georgia would hold onto its history of white supremacy and fight desegregation.

Some said the 1956 flag was adopted in honor of the 100th anniversary of the Civil War, which was still five years away. However, evidence shows it was created in response to the federal government's efforts to end segregation.

CHAPTER FIVE

THE SIBLEY COMMISSION

The outcry against integrating schools in Georgia was so great that, in 1960, the state put together a committee to decide whether to desegregate public schools or close them. The committee was called the Sibley Commission, because it was headed by a lawyer from Atlanta named John Sibley.

John Sibley believed in segregation but felt that no matter how much state governments resisted desegregation, the federal government would enforce it in the end. Sibley held public hearings across the state to determine how people thought the state government should proceed. Most of those who attended Sibley's hearings wanted total segregation to continue. However, the Sibley Commission found that resisting the federal law would only create greater problems for the state government. In 1961, the government approved the commission's plan, which ended full segregation in schools but also gave them ways to slow integration.

In January 1961, a federal judge ordered that two black students be admitted to the University of Georgia. There were riots at the university by those resisting integration.

CHAPTER SIX

MARTIN LUTHER KING JR.

Martin Luther King Jr. was the most famous leader of the civil rights movement. King was born in Atlanta, Georgia, and attended Morehouse College there. After he married Coretta Scott in 1953, King moved to Montgomery, Alabama, where he worked as a minister in a Baptist church. In Montgomery, King became involved in the civil rights movement during the Montgomery bus **boycott**, which started in December 1955.

The Montgomery bus boycott lasted for 381 days. It resulted in the integration of Montgomery city buses.

The bus boycott was sparked by the arrest of Rosa Parks, a woman who refused to give up her seat on a segregated bus to a white man.

After the boycott, King helped form the Southern Christian Leadership Conference, also called the SCLC, in Atlanta, Georgia. He acted as president and led many nonviolent **campaigns** to end segregation and register black voters. The SCLC brought many Christian African Americans together. Leaders organized nonviolent protests such as marches, boycotts, and sit-ins.

CHAPTER SEVEN

THE SNCC

Nonviolent protests were an important part of the civil rights movement. Through peaceful demonstrations, activists raised awareness about issues of racial discrimination and segregation. Often these protests were met with violence from the police. This mistreatment of peaceful protestors caused an outcry in more integrated northern cities and helped earn sympathy for the movement.

Activists formed the Student Nonviolent Coordinating Committee in 1960. Better known as SNCC, this organization was devoted to racial integration and other social change. The SNCC gave young people more of a voice in the civil rights movement.

Atlanta, Georgia, was a hot spot for SNCC action. The many students attending black colleges there joined the SNCC to peacefully fight against injustice. They staged protests at Atlanta department stores. Ivan Allen Jr., the mayor of Atlanta from 1962 to 1970, proved to be an important ally to the civil rights cause. He made many strides toward desegregation. In 1966, the SNCC created the Atlanta Project to address the issues in the black community there.

The SCLC and the SNCC were made up of both African American and white members. This photo shows members of the SNCC.

CHAPTER EIGHT

THE ALBANY MOVEMENT

In late 1961, local African Americans attempted to desegregate the city of Albany, Georgia. The Albany Movement was the first attempt to desegregate an entire community. SNCC members organized sit-ins and marches to protest the segregation they experienced daily in Albany. By mid-December, over 500 civil rights activists had been arrested in Albany.

About this time, Martin Luther King Jr. arrived in Albany to lend his help to the movement. Protestors hoped that his participation would draw news attention and national support. After he spoke at a meeting in Albany, King was arrested and imprisoned. This happened a number of times over the course of the movement, which lasted until August 1962. The Albany Movement did not result in the immediate end of segregation. However, it did inspire other cities, and Albany's facilities were desegregated only a year later.

Antisegregation activists were often arrested. Mass arrests helped gain national attention for the civil rights movement. This photo shows Martin Luther King Jr. after an arrest.

CHAPTER NINE

MARCH ON WASHINGTON

In summer 1963, Martin Luther King Jr. and other civil rights leaders organized a march to call attention to the issue of black unemployment, job and wage discrimination, and overall issues of racial discrimination and segregation. The SCLC, SNCC, Congress of Racial Equality, and National Association for the Advancement of Colored People were among the many organizations that took part in the event. Georgia was well represented by King and many other Georgian civil rights activists.

In his "I Have a Dream" speech, King said he had hope for an America free from segregation and discrimination. The March on Washington took place nearly 100 years after Abraham Lincoln made the **Emancipation Proclamation**.

This photo shows President John F. Kennedy meeting with civil rights leaders at the White House in 1963.

Over 200,000 people marched through the nation's capital to the Lincoln Memorial, where the crowd sang songs and leaders made speeches. It was during the March on Washington that King made his famous "I Have a Dream" speech. The civil rights leaders met with President John F. Kennedy and Vice President Lyndon B. Johnson to discuss civil rights legislation. This laid the foundation for the Civil Rights Act of 1964.

CHAPTER TEN

THE 1964 CIVIL RIGHTS ACT

On July 2, 1964, President Lyndon B. Johnson signed the Civil Rights Act into law. President Kennedy originally proposed the Civil Rights Act, but Congress strongly resisted it. Kennedy was **assassinated** in 1963, and Vice President Johnson followed him as president. During his term, Johnson urged Congress to pass the Civil Rights Act.

The Civil Rights Act of 1964 marked the end of legal segregation in public places. It also made it illegal for companies to discriminate based on race, color, sex, religion, and national origin when hiring employees. It was a huge victory for the civil rights movement because it promised equal access to public facilities and equal employment opportunities. The Civil Rights Act was followed by the Voting Rights Act of 1965, which aimed to protect voters from discrimination. Unfortunately, these new laws were met with resistance in Georgia.

The Civil Rights Act of 1964 was a major step toward making segregation illegal. This photo shows President Johnson signing the act. Martin Luther King Jr. is visible behind him.

CHAPTER ELEVEN

KING AND LEWIS

Voting rights for African Americans were one of the main civil rights issues in Georgia. Martin Luther King Jr. and the SCLC worked with John Lewis, a leader of the SNCC, to organize a campaign in Selma, Alabama, to protect the voting rights of southern blacks.

In early 1965, Lewis helped organize a march from Selma, Alabama, to the state capital, Montgomery. The march was a 54-mile (86.9 km) journey to call attention to issues surrounding African American voting rights and police treatment of peaceful protestors.

As the marchers were leaving Selma, they were stopped by state troopers who ordered them to go home. The troopers beat the peaceful protesters with clubs and whips. John Lewis was among the many people who were injured in the attack. This incident came to be called "Bloody Sunday."

John Lewis won a seat on the Atlanta City Council in 1981. Georgia voters elected him to the House of Representatives in 1986. He has served in Congress ever since.

CHAPTER TWELVE

RESPONSE TO CIVIL RIGHTS PROGRESS

Unfortunately, the Civil Rights Act didn't end segregation and discrimination. In Georgia, as in many other southern states, politicians resisted the federal laws put in place to protect African Americans.

Lester Maddox took office as the governor of Georgia in 1967. Before entering politics, Maddox was the owner of a restaurant at which he refused to serve African Americans, even after the Civil Rights Act. When three African American

This photo shows Maddox outside of his restaurant in 1962. An African American man protests the restaurant while white supporters carry signs promoting Maddox.

In 1974, Maddox unsuccessfully ran for governor again. He ran for president in 1976.

civil rights activists tried to visit Maddox's restaurant in 1964, he forced them out and threatened them. Maddox eventually closed his restaurant rather than allow black customers.

As a politician, Maddox continued to support segregation. Even though he couldn't change the Civil Rights Act, he did his best to delay its effects in Georgia. He opposed many federal plans to improve civil rights.

CHAPTER THIRTEEN

CONTINUING THE FIGHT

The Civil Rights Act of 1964 and Voting Rights Act of 1965 didn't solve many of the problems faced by African American Georgians. Many lived in poor communities and lacked better housing. Many people suffered violence at the hands of the police and were unable to find jobs. Discrimination continued to keep many black Georgians from improving their lives and from achieving representation in government. From 1965 to 1970, a number of race riots occurred in cities such as Atlanta and Augusta.

Georgia's history of slavery and segregation created an economic divide between white and black Georgians that slowed the effects of the civil rights movement. Racial divisions in Georgia continued to cause problems.

In 1968, Congress passed the Fair Housing Act, which made it illegal to discriminate against people buying or renting homes based on their race, color, religion, or national origin.

Many consider 1968 to be the end of the classic civil rights movement. However, people still fight for civil rights today.

CHAPTER FOURTEEN

A NEW TIME

The classic civil rights movement spanned more than a decade, beginning in 1954 and ending in 1968. It cost many activists their lives, including Martin Luther King Jr., who was assassinated in Memphis, Tennessee, in 1968. Without the struggle of thousands of activists during the 1950s and 1960s, racial segregation might still exist in the United States.

Although great strides were made during the movement, full racial equality has not been achieved in Georgia or in all of the United States. For the most part, African Americans do not have equal representation in the state or federal governments. Discrimination and unequal access to education and employment opportunities continue to limit the freedoms of many African American citizens. Racial discrimination affects people every day. It's important to be aware that the fight to guarantee and protect the civil rights of all citizens is an ongoing struggle in the United States.

GLOSSARY

activist (AK-tih-vist) Someone who acts strongly in support of or against an issue.

assassinate (uh-SA-suh-nayt) To kill someone, especially a public figure.

boycott (BOY-kaht) To join with others in refusing to buy from or deal with a person, nation, or business.

campaign (kam-PAYN) A series of actions to bring about a certain result, such as winning an election.

discrimination (dis-krih-muh-NAY-shun) Different–usually unfair–treatment based on factors such as a person's race, age, religion, or gender.

Emancipation Proclamation (ih-man-sih-PAY-shun prak-luh-MAY-shun) The piece of writing issued by Abraham Lincoln that said slaves in Confederate states were free.

enact (uh-NAKT) To put into place or bring about.

enforce (en-FORS) To make people do or not do something.

facility (fuh-SIH-luh-tee) Buildings that are built for a certain purpose.

segregation (seh-gruh-GAY-shun) The separation of people based on race, class, or ethnicity.

white supremacist (WYT suh-PREH-muh-sist) A person who believes that white people are better than all other people.

INDEX

PRIMARY SOURCE LIST

Page 7 *At the bus station in Durham, North Carolina*. Photograph by Jack Delano. May 1940. Now kept at the Library of Congress's Prints and Photographs division, Washington, D.C.

Page 9 *Brown v. Board of Education* judgment, 1954. Supreme Court document. Now kept at the National Archives and Records Administration, Records of the Supreme Court, Record Group 267, National Archives Identifier: 301669.

Page 23 President Lyndon B. Johnson signing the 1964 Civil Rights Act. Photograph by Cecil Stoughton. July 2, 1940. Now kept at the White House Press Office, Washington, D.C.

WEBSITES

Due to the changing nature of Internet links, PowerKids Press has developed an online list of websites related to the subject of this book. This site is updated regularly. Please use this link to access the list: www.powerkidslinks.com/sog/civ